文・タケシタナカ
絵・小島伸吾
監修・桜雲会／馬場景子

闇を照らした白い花

斎藤百合の生涯とヘレン・ケラー

　小つるの小さな手が、井戸の縁に必死にしがみついていました。
「ギャー　ギャー　ギャー　ギャー」
　火がついたようなさけび声が、井戸に共鳴して暗闇に響きわたっていました。
　そのときです。人のものとは思えない何か不思議な力が、井戸の奥底から小つるの小さなからだを押しあげたのです。
「おぉー……、わしは、なんてことを……、なんて恐ろしいことを……、すまん、すまん……」
　小つるの父親は、3歳になるわが子を抱きしめ、井戸のそばで泣きくずれました。
　のちに、ヘレン・ケラーの影響を受けて、日本の「盲女子の母」と慕われるようになる斎藤百合は、このとき生まれたのかもしれません。

　小つるは、1891年、石巻山（今の愛知県豊橋市）の麓にあるとても小さな村で生まれました。
　両親は、祖父母に小つるを預け、旅回りの浪曲師をしていました。
　麻疹で、子どもがどんどん死んでいった時代です。小つるも3歳のときにかかってしまいました。
　なんとか命は助かったものの、高熱と栄養失調により、失明してしまいます。
　旅から帰ってきた父親は、
「目が見えなくて生きていくなんて、辛いだけだ」
　行く末を案じ、小つるを井戸に投げ込もうとしたのです。

光を失った小つるは、それでも元気に成長していきます。でも、学校に行くことはできません。
　いつも石巻山の麓の原っぱで、学校から帰ってくる友だちを待ち受けています。
「今日は、どんな勉強したん？」
　学校のことが知りたくてたまりません。
「じゃ、今から今日習ったところ読むから、聞いとりん」
　小つるは、じっと聞いています。
「わたしに読ませておくれん」
　小つるは、教科書を手に持ってスラスラと読んでみせます。
「あれ、小つるちゃんの教科書逆さまだがぁ」
　みんな、大笑い。

　こんなこともありました。
　その日は、友だちが学校でやった踊りを教えてくれていました。
　小つるは、いつにもまして真剣。一つひとつの振り付けを手と指先でしっかり確認していると、
「そんなにさわったら、くすぐったいがぁ」
　歌も教えてくれました。
　小つるは、すぐに覚えてしまいます。
　手拍子をとりながら歌い、踊り、なかなかさまになっています。

ある日の夕暮れ、いつものように原っぱであそんでいると。
「あれ、いい匂い！どこに咲いてるの？」
　夕方の少し冷んやりした空気のなかに咲く花の香りは、とても甘くて可憐。
　小つるは、花の香りにさそわれ、みんなからはなれていきます。
（あぁ、この花ね）
　花弁にそっと人差し指をすべらせました。
「みんな、この花は何？　ねえ」
　辺りはもうすっかり日が暮れていました。
　しゃがみこんで花の香りを楽しんでいた小つるは、みんなが帰ってしまったことに気づきませんでした。
「だれもおらんのかん」
　その場でグルグルグルグル。
　どれくらい時間が経ったでしょう。

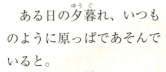

「小つる！…小つる！」
「おばあちゃん！、おばあちゃーん」
　泣きじゃくりながら声のする方向に走りました。
　あせったので、何度もころんでしまいました。
「よかった、よかった、さぞ怖かったらぁ」
　抱きおこしてくれたおばあちゃんのざらざらの大きな手は、とても温かでした。
　冷えていた小つるの背中で、おばあちゃんが涙をぬぐっているのがわかりました。
「おばあちゃん、この花、何？　なんて名前？」
「これは、まっ白い百合の花だよ、いい匂いだらぁ」

目が見えない小つるの世界では、まわりのみんなの話し声やみんなとつないでいる手が、明かりを感じさせてくれています。
　小つるは、まわりにだれもいない恐怖をこのときはじめて知ったのです。

　小つるは9歳になっていました。
　明治時代の末です。たいていの子どもたちは尋常小学校を卒業すると働きに出ます。
　小つるは、豊橋の按摩師のもとに修業に出ることになりました。

「がんばるんだよ」
　小つるの母は、小つるを送って村はずれまでくると、紙に包んだ小つるの好物の黒砂糖の塊を小さな手に握らせ、振り返ることもなく小走りにもどってしまいました。

　按摩の修業といっても家事からはじまりました。そのほかは、ほぼ一年間、板や畳を揉むことだけでした。指先を強くするためです。

　ところが、10歳になった小つるは、両親といっしょに岐阜の町にいました。
　父親の浪花節に合わせて三味線を弾きながら歩く母親。そして、小つるも母親の揺れる袂を握りながら浪花節を口ずさんで、歩いていました。
　踊りや歌をすぐに覚えることのできる小つるには、按摩より合っていると考えて、小つるの両親が豊橋から連れもどしたのです。

「旅回りの芸人さんだね」
　男の人が一家に声をかけてきました。そこは「岐阜聖公会訓盲院」と書かれた建物の前でした。
　その人の目は忙しく瞬いています。
「急に声をかけて驚かせてしまったね。ここは盲人のための訓練所ですよ。わたしは、院長の森巻耳といいます。もし、まちがいだったら、すみませんね。娘さんは、目が見えないんじゃないかい」
　小つるは、その声に、今までに感じたことのない優しさと親しみを覚えました。

「見てのとおりわたしも盲人です。目が見えないと、ほかの感覚がさえていましてね」
「こんな旅の毎日、娘には、とてもかわいそうな思いをさせています」
「娘さんは何歳になりますか」
「もう10歳になります……。名前は小つるといいます」
「目の見えないお子さんをお連れになって旅するのは大変でしょう。小つるさんを、この訓盲院にお預けになりませんか」
「えっ！」
と、父親。
　突然の申し出に、小つるの父親も母親もそのあとの言葉がでません。
「心配しなくて大丈夫です。ここで娘さんはたくさんのことを学べます。会いたいときにはいつでも会いに来てください」

　両親は、森巻耳院長の温和な人柄と誠意を感じて、小つるを預けることにしました。

岐阜聖公会訓盲院で、小つるは一番年下でした。
　敬虔なクリスチャンだった森院長は、活発で聡明な小つるを、わが子のように可愛がりました。
　ここでも按摩教育がおこなわれましたが、そのやり方は、豊橋の修業とはまったくことなっていました。マッサージの理論にのっとった技術訓練がおこなわれていました。もともと器用な小つるは、のみこみも早く、ようやく豊橋の辛い修業も役立ちました。
　全額給費生として鍼や按摩を学んでいた小つるは、宣教師とともに外国人の家庭に招かれて、オルガンを弾くこともありました。もともと両親の影響で音感がよかったので、簡単な曲は、すぐに弾けるようになっていたのです。そして、英会話も身につけていきます。

　小つるは、点字とも出会っていました。
　はじめて指先で触れたボツボツした盛り上がり。それが、小つるの人生を切り開く恩物になったのです。
「これは何？」
　6つの点で表される文字の世界があることを知ったときの小つるの喜びようは、あっという間に点字を覚えたことが証明しました。
　点訳本の読書は、小つるの生活を豊かにしてくれました。
　小つるはしだいに、
（一人でも多くの盲人に点訳本を紹介したい！）
と、思うようになりました。

　17歳になった小つるは、訓盲院の代用教員になりました。
　そして、この年に聖公会の按手礼を受けてクリスチャンとして生きることを誓いました。これは、我が子同然に育ててきた森院長夫妻の願いでもありました。
　小つるは、代用教員としてもらった給料のほとんどを点訳に費やしました。とくに熱心に取り組んだ「讃美歌」や、ヘレン・ケラーの本でした。
（目が見えないだけでなく、耳も聞こえない女性が、学問を修め、障害者だけでなくあらゆる人に勇気を与えている）
　ヘレン・ケラーの生き方は小つるの心の支えとなっていました。
　小つるは、自分で点字を読むだけでなく、いろいろな人たちからあらゆる書物を読んで聞かせてもらいました。なかには、英語の本も多くありました。小つるの英語力は、どんどんのびていきます。

The White Flower To Brighten The Darkness

Saito Yuri's Life and Helen Keller

P1

Kotsuru's tiny hand was desperately grasping the edge of the well.
"Wah, wah, wah, wah!!"
Her heartrending, piteous wails pierced the darkness, echoing up from the gloom of the well.
And then, that was the moment. It was nothing like a human, a strange force.....
A strange force seemed to push Kotsuru's small body away from the edge.
"Oh no! What...what terrible thing have I done? I'm so sorry....so sorry."
Kotsuru's father hugged his 3-year-old daughter to his chest and collapsed in tears at the side of the well.
That was probably the moment when Saito Yuri, later to be inspired by Helen Keller and become Japan's much loved "Mother of Blind Women", was born.

Kotsuru came into this world in 1891 in a small village nestled at the foot of Mt. Ishimaki (present day Toyohashi City in Aichi Prefecture).
Her parents were wandering musical minstrels and left the young Kotsuru with her grandparents.
It was a time when many children died from measles. Kotsuru also caught the disease when she was 3 years old.
Luckily she survived but, due to a high temperature and malnutrition, she lost her eyesight.
On returning from his travels, her father had said,
" To survive but to be blind....there is only suffering ahead."
Anxious about her future, he had tried to throw his young child into the well.

P2

Despite the loss of her sight, Kotsuru grew up a healthy, cheerful child. However, she was unable to go to school.
Every day, in a field below Mt. Ishimaki, Kotsuru waited for her friends to return from school.
"What did you study today?"
She couldn't wait to hear everything about the school day.
"OK, I'll read what we learned today, listen carefully---"
Kotsuru listened intently.
"Now let me read it, please."
Kotsuru took the textbook in her hands and read it smoothly.
"Ah, Kotsuru's text book is upside down!"
They all laughed loudly.

Then one day, the following happened.
Her friends were teaching her a dance they had learned at school that day.
Kotsuru was even more attentive than usual. She carefully followed each movement they made with her hands and fingertips.
"Ah, touching me like that makes me ticklish!!"
They also taught her songs.
Kotsuru quickly learned them all.
Clapping to keep time, she could sing and dance very well.

P3

One evening at dusk, they were playing as usual in the open field.
"Oh, what a beautiful smell. Where's that flower blooming?"
The sweet scent of the flower wafted through the cool evening air.
Led away by the scent of the flower, Kotsuru soon became separated from her friends.
"Ah, this is it."
She softly slid her forefinger over the petal of the flower.
"Hey, everyone, what flower is this? Hey...."
All around her the daylight had completely faded.
Squatting down and enjoying the touch and smell of the flower, Kotsuru hadn't noticed that her friends had all gone home.
"Hey, is anyone there? Anyone....."
She stumbled round and round in circles. How long was she wandering for?

"Kotsuru!! Kotsuru!!"
"Grandma!! Grandma!!"
With tears streaming down her face, she ran to the sound of the voice.
Rushing, she fell down many times.
"Oh thank goodness, thank goodness. You must have been terrified!"
Her grandmother's large, rough hands felt so warm as she picked Kotsuru up and held her close.
Shivering, she felt her grandmother wipe tears away on her shoulder.
"Grandma, what's this flower? What is it called?"
"That's a white lily. Doesn't it have a beautiful smell?"

P4

In Kotsuru's world without sight, it was the voices of those around her and the hands that held hers that allowed her to feel the brightness.
This was the first time she had ever felt the dread of being left on her own.

Kotsuru became 9 years old. That time was the end of the Meiji period and it was usual that most children of that age left their regular elementary school

and started work.
It was decided that Kotsuru would go to train under a masseur in Toyohashi.

"Do your best!"
Kotsuru's mother came with them to the edge of the village to see her off, pressed a chunk of Kotsuru's favorite black sugar wrapped in paper into her little hand then hurried back down the little street without once looking over her shoulder.
Though they said she was there to learn to be a masseur, her training started with doing just the housework.
Other than that, all she did for about the first year was practice massaging floorboards and tatami mats in order to strengthen her fingertips.

P5

However, when Kotsuru was 10 years old, she was with her parents in a town in Gifu Prefecture.
Kotsuru's father told naniwabushi, musical stories, accompanied by her mother playing the shamisen.
Kotsuru walked with them, gripping her mother's sleeve and humming along to her father's stories.
Knowing how quickly she could learn to sing and dance, her parents had taken her back from Toyohashi to be with them, thinking this would be more suitable for her than massage.

"So, you are wandering minstrels?"
A man spoke to them as they passed in front of a building on which hung a sign saying, Gifu Anglican Training Center for the Blind.
The man's eyes blinked rapidly.
"I hope I didn't surprise you too much by suddenly speaking. This is a training place for the blind. I'm the principle of the Center, Mori Kenji. Forgive me if I am mistaken, but your daughter is blind, isn't she?"
Kotsuru felt that she had never before heard a voice so full of such kindness and friendliness.

"As you can, I'm blind too. When one can't see, the other senses become sharper."
"We do feel sorry for our daughter, traveling around like this every day."
"How old is she now?"
"She's already 10 years old....... Her name is Kotsuru."
"It must be very difficult for you bringing your blind daughter along with you on your travels.
Why not leave Kotsuru here at this training place for the blind?"
"Eh?" exclaimed Kotsuru's father.
On suddenly being presented with such an offer, Kotsuru's parents were lost for words.
"It's all right, there's no cause to be worried. Your daughter will be able to learn many things here and you can come to see her anytime you wish."

Kotsuru's parents were deeply moved by Principle Mori's gentle personality and sincerity and decided to leave Kotsuru in his care.

P6

Kotsuru was the youngest student at the Center.
Seeing how active and bright she was, the devoutly Christian Principal Mori cherished Kotsuru as if she was his own child.
Massage skills were also studied here but the training was very different to what she had experienced in Toyohashi. Here, techniques conforming to the massage were practiced. Kotsuru, being skillful by nature, learned quickly and was finally able to make use of the severe training she had endured in Toyohashi.
While studying acupuncture and massage as a full scholarship student, Kotsuru also got to play the organ when she was invited to the houses of foreigners along with missionaries from the school. Having a fine sense of pitch from the influence of her parents, Kotsuru was soon able to play simple tunes. What's more, she started to acquire English conversation on these visits.

This was when Kotsuru came to know braille.
She felt immense excitement when she first ran her fingertips over the raised points and it became a gift that opened up her life.
"What is this?"
She was so delighted when she found out there was a world where letters could be represented by 6 raised points that she mastered braille in no time at all.
Reading books written in braille enriched Kotsuru's life.
She came to think that she wanted to introduce braille books to as many blind people as possible.

When she was 17, Kotsuru became a substitute teacher at the Gifu Center for the Blind.
Then, also in that year, she was accepted into the Anglican faith and vowed to live her life as a Christian. This was something that Mr. and Mrs. Mori, having raised her as if she was their own child, had wished for her.
Kotsuru spent most of the salary she earned on braille translations, in particular hymnals and books by Helen Keller.
"A woman who not only cannot see but also cannot hear yet completes her academic studies gives courage to all people, not only the disabled."
The way Helen Keller lived her life would always be a source of great strength and support to Kotsuru's heart.
Kotsuru not only read braille herself, she also had other people read a variety of books to her. Among these were many English books and Kotsuru's English ability continued to improve.

P8

When Kotsuru read Helen Keller's 1902 book, "The Story of My Life", she learned that their lives were completely opposite, Helen had been brought up in a very prosperous household and had been extremely spoilt.
• Helen was born in 1880 so she's 11 years older than me.
• She lost her sight from an illness like me.

- But she also lost her hearing!
- And she couldn't speak!!
- What can that be like?
- Being unable to hear, you can't hear your own voice.
- Also you can't hear any other sounds you make.
- Of course you won't be able to speak.

Considering these things, naturally Kotsuru took a deep interest in Helen. She would always imagine meeting Helen one day:
Kotsuru would touch Helen's face. Helen would touch Kotsuru's face, too. Being unable to hear, Helen would feel for Kotsuru's face more intensely.

Kotsuru also learned the following things.
- Helen's parents were close to Graham Bell, well known as the inventor of the telephone.
- Bell introduced them to the principal of the Massachusetts State School for the Blind who had one of his graduates, the then 20-year old Anne Sullivan, go to the Keller house to be a home tutor for Helen.
- Having had weak eyesight since she was small, Sullivan made use of her own experience to teach Helen sign language and words. She also trained the spoilt, selfish Helen in good behavior and manners.
- One day Helen understood that the cold thing she had touched was called "water" and it was represented by writing the letters WATER.
- Sullivan also taught her how to move her mouth to pronounce the word "water".
- From this starting point, Helen learned that all things had names and that by moving her mouth in the appropriate way, she could let other people know what she was thinking.

P9

In 1890, Helen studied how to use her voice at the Boston School for the Deaf.
In addition, in 1894 she enrolled in the New York School for the Deaf and worked intensely on vocal training exercises.
This was the time that Kotsuru was born, and in the same way as Helen, she later lost her sight to illness.
In October 1900, Helen enrolled in Radcliffe College, present day Harvard University.

After working as a substitute teacher for 3 years, Principal Mori acknowledged Kotsuru's talents and enrolled her on the teaching course of the Acupuncture Department at the Tokyo School for the Blind, as a transfer student from the Gifu Training Center.
The costs of her transfer were covered by contributions or payments for home treatment.
Having made it possible for Kotsuru to take this momentous step, Principal Mori had expectations of her so great they were almost beyond words.

Her life at the Tokyo School for the Blind was like a dream come true for Kotsuru.
There were 9 students in her class of whom 7 were male. She was one of only 2 female students. They were all the excellent students who had transferred from Schools for the Blind located throughout the country. They were each expected to be the future driving force behind their respective schools.

During this time, Kotsuru completed a copy of an English-Japanese dictionary in braille.
In total there were 8 volumes and on each volume was her pen name.
"White Lily"
Yes, that's right, the brilliant "white lily" from that time long ago.

P10

"Whatever the case may be, marriage is not something for blind girls to hope for. This is because there is absolutely no way they can fulfill the responsibilities of a wife and mother. If they are considering marriage, they must be strictly warned against it and not allowed to marry."
This was written in a book entitled "Education For The Blind".
However, it was not surprising that Kotsuru felt differently to this way of thinking as she had already acquired a wide-ranging education and understood the state of the outside world, particularly from an American viewpoint.
Kotsuru thought, "All people are equal. It's important to cooperate while acknowledging our differences."

This was the Kotsuru who fell in love. Her partner was Saito Takeya, a fellow student 2 classes below her. Unlike Kotsuru, who was completely blind, Takeya only suffered from diminished eyesight.

In 1913, the Meiji era gave way to the Taisho period. In this year, Kotsuru was to graduate from the Tokyo School for the Blind.
Having come to Tokyo on a full scholarship as a transfer student from the Gifu Training Center for the Blind, it was required that she return to the Center to become a leader there.
So, Kotsuru planned and carried out an outrageous action. She took Takeya's masseur and acupuncturist license.
"This is proof of our engagement," she said and took the license back with her to Gifu.
She felt it necessary to take such an extreme action as she was worried that she wouldn't see Takeya again.

P11

It was a long time since she had been at the Center.
Back from Tokyo she had a glamourous aura about her to Principal Mori and the students.
They were all excited and expectant at the prospect of knowing all the things she had gained in Tokyo.
Hence, they were astonished by what Kotsuru told them.
"I plan to marry Saito Takeya, one of my fellow students at the Tokyo School for the Blind."
"What do you mean?" asked Principal Mori.
His voice was calm and quiet, but he trembled and inside he was anxious because his plan had always been to entrust the future of the Center to the capable leadership of Kotsuru.

But Kotsuru was unable to see how he felt.

"I know it's selfish of me Principal Mori, please forgive me. But, whatever happens, I want to marry Mr. Saito."

Kotsuru's strong determination was clearly expressed in her direct, strong tone of voice.

However, while being aware of the strength in Kotsuru's voice, Principal Mori was unable to see her expression. In the face of the forcefulness in her voice, the only thing he could do was to allow the marriage.

Having had her desire to marry Takeya accepted, for 2 years, from 1913 to 1915, Kotsuru devoted herself to working without rest at the Center to repay all the kindness she had received in the past.

And then, in the autumn of 1915, she married Saito Takeya, by then a masseur at a hospital in Tokyo. They started their new life in a new home in Zoshigaya in Tokyo.

On the opportunity presented by their marriage, Kotsuru took the name Saito Yuri.

P12

For Yuri, who had never known a normal family life as she was growing up, every day of her new life with Takeya was filled with happiness, even as she struggled with unfamiliar housework.

She got used to taking the street to go shopping, the street to the public bath and the crowded roads around Tokyo. She could even sometimes go to meet Takeya at the station and eventually she wasn't worried about walking around by herself.

In time, she became pregnant.

One day, as she was walking she was aware of a man speaking to her as he passed by.

"Oi, you're a masseuse, aren't you? Now, whose is that kid you've got inside you, heh?" he laughingly mocked her, his words full of contempt.

Yuri felt light-headed and almost stumbled, but, after pulling herself together, she was finally able to find her way home.

"I'm sorry, I'm sorry!"

Yuri cried and couldn't stop stroking her stomach as she apologized over and over to her unborn child.

"Because I'm blind, people even make fun of my child. I don't care about me but it's really unkind to my baby," she thought to herself.

P13

Just then, Takeya came back home.

"Yuri, did something happen to you?" he asked.

Yuri clung tightly to Takeya and through her tears, she blurted out what had taken place on the street.

After hearing her story, Takeya spoke gently to her.

"Now, listen Yuri. That baby you are carrying is our wish, our dream. It's also the hope for society in the future."

Silently, Yuri nodded her head in agreement.

"It's true that in this world there are many blind girls who can't even say the names of their parents. Therefore, we must do all we can to bring up this child properly. We have to change society's prejudice towards blind women. Now, pull yourself together, young mother."

While saying this, Takeya blew softly on Yuri's stomach and the warmth seemed to spread throughout her body and deep into her heart.

The events of that day would cause Yuri to think deeply about the low status of blind women in society.

In August 1916, Yuri gave birth to her first daughter, Kumi.

P14

Every morning, Takeya would use a magnifying glass and read the day's news from the newspaper to Yuri. These 30 minutes were an important source of information for her. It was her window on the world.

One day, there was something in the news that would cause a big change in Yuri's life.

"Tokyo Women's University will open in 1918. The aim is to provide higher education for women with a Christian foundation."

"Eh? Can you read that again?"

Yuri couldn't conceal her excitement.

"But....no, it's nothing to do with me. It's impossible. I'm already 26. I'm blind. On top of that, I've got a baby....and we couldn't pay the school fees..... and....."

Yuri's initial excitement disappeared as she tried to convince herself with all the reasons against the idea.

"Don't give up before you even begin. Let's get some more details."

With this encouragement from Takeya, Yuri sent away for an application form.

There was an oral examination to enter the University. Her interviewer was Yasui Tetsu, who would later become the second President of Tokyo Women's University.

"This is a school for women who intend to study. You are already married. You are a mother and what's more, you are unable to see. Still, do you think you can keep up with your studies?"

With such a severe enquiry being the first thing out of his mouth, Yuri became agitated.

"Even if someone is blind, they should have an equal chance to get an education. In order to improve the lowly status of blind women in society, it's necessary to increase the number of people who are able to receive a higher education. First, give me that chance."

Yuri appealed defiantly to Mr. Yasui in this way. But then she thought, "Oh no, I made a mistake, I said too much", and in her mind gave up on passing the exam. However, a few days later, she received notification that she had been successful in the test.

P15

The first President of Tokyo Women's University was Nitobe Inazo, who, having dedicated his life to promoting world peace, described himself as "a bridge across the Pacific". He had a deep understanding of disabled people and their problems.

Yuri's passion had come across clearly to him. Yasui Tetsu's strict questioning had also been used to check Yuri's determination.
"I can go to university!"
Later, Mr. Yasui would become truly sympathetic to Yuri's cause and a firm supporter of her actions in many ways.

In the lecture hall, Yuri always sat at the very front. Never wanting to miss a word of the lectures, the image of her intently taking notes in braille gave a wonderfully eager impression to her classmates.
They were so moved because, in those days, very few people had ever seen braille and now they were watching somebody using it right in front of them. Sometimes the person sitting next to her would read out what was written on the blackboard.
Yuri quickly became very popular at the university. Even so, everyone's generous cooperation, as she took lectures with her baby strapped to her back or sitting silently on the seat next to her, was probably due above all to the kind of person Yuri was.

Graduation was approaching, but Yuri was keen to continue studying. She wanted to study English.
In 1923, Yuri enrolled in the English literature department.
However, on September 1st of that year, the Great Kanto Earthquake occurred. After the earthquake, the streets of Tokyo were completely changed. This made it very dangerous for Yuri to walk anywhere and it was unavoidable that she had to drop out of university.
Nevertheless, in 1925 Yuri enrolled on a postgraduate course in the department of English literature at the Tokyo School for the Blind and continued her studies. Takeya also took classes in social policy at night school while continuing to work during the day. Of course, their household finances were in dire straits. But their life seemed full and busy as, due to their bright, cheerful nature, there were often people coming to visit them.
For Yuri and Takeya, who were studying to improve the status of blind and disabled people in society, bringing up their child was never used as an excuse to neglect their studies.

P16

One of Takeya's friends from his time at the Tokyo School for the Blind was a Russian, Vasily Yeroshenko. He had come to research the situation in Japan where blind people were using their massage and acupuncture skills to maintain their independence and he had a wide circle of friends.
He often invited Takeya and Yuri to gatherings where each time, they met artists and writers and engaged in heated discussions about their desire for a new era. Sometimes Yeroshenko played the violin, Yuri accompanied him on the organ and the others joined in and sang along with them.

P17

But this was the time of the so-called Taisho Democracy and the police maintained strict supervision of such meetings. Under these conditions, the atmosphere at such gatherings was a strange mixture of the heart being liberated and free and of feeling confined in an enclosed space.
Yeroshenko was eventually deported as he was considered a "person of dangerous thoughts". This happened on the day Yuri and Takeya were attending Easter services.
As all these things took place, they continued to try to improve the status of blind people in society and struggled to get by as they published many braille books at their own expense.

P18

In November 1928, Yuri formed the Musashino Women's Group, later to be called The Sunlight Women's Group (Yokofujinkai). Then, in 1930, she established the Sunlight Association (Yokokai), for the benefit of blind girls.
The principle behind this group was as follows:
"We cannot see the sun but it shines on all the people in the world. Blind people shouldn't be on the edges of society. We must make a society where even blind people have equal access to education."
The Sunlight Association depended on a quarterly magazine that Takeya had started called "Braille Club" for its operation. The contents of the magazine were a diverse range of articles about art and literature, problems facing blind people, current affairs and contributions from readers. It was a valuable resource for many readers, particularly blind people from other regions, and the number of subscribers who eagerly awaited its arrival was increasing. And Yuri was more and more energetic and active!
In December of 1935, she hung a brand new sign at the entrance of an old house in Toshima Ward's Zoshigaya bearing the words "The Sunlight Association Home". Yuri received support from many people, including Yasui Tetsu, the President of Tokyo Women's University, and Honma Kazuo, who would become the first director of The Japan Braille Library.
"Braille Club" was also published from the Home. The tap, tap, tap of braille being written and the clanging of the printing machines echoed far and wide and the sounds of student volunteers reading aloud and young people laughing could be heard coming from the humble, 2-storey house.
People would stop and stare as they were passing by and ask, "What kind of a house is this?"
It was a house of learning for young blind women.
Yuri's life had been opened up on meeting Principal Mori of The Gifu Anglican Training Center for the Blind. Now it was her turn to bestow on the blind women she met the same affection that Mr. Mori had shown to her.
However, as the number of people gathering there increased, covering the maintenance of the Home just on issues of "Braille Club" became more and more difficult. They started to cover operating costs by becoming agents for the sale of braille equipment

or paper and treatment implements.

Meanwhile, there was a continuous stream of people coming up to Tokyo from the provinces and depending on Yuri. She offered these women a warm welcome and provided them with food and lodging.

This was how Yuri came to be called "The Mother of Blind Women".

By the entrance to the Home stood an old camellia tree and it was a beautiful sight when its flowers were in full bloom.

P19

In 1936, the February 26th Incident occurred. The Marco Polo Bridge Incident took place on July 7th, 1937. All-out war broke out between Japan and China. As conditions continued to worsen in Japanese society, Yuri's ideals didn't change.

"I long for the day when blind women can be seen working side by side with sighted people. To achieve that, we must develop people who will be leaders in 20 or 30 years time."

Before she knew it, the dream of opening an institution called "The Blind Girls' High School" was growing in her.

In the December 1937 issue of "Braille Club", Yuri published a major article entitled "Seeking Student Applications for the "The Blind Girls' High School".

"Our goal is to train people to be the core of blind women's society. The curriculum will consist of the following classes: history of Western philosophy, history of Japanese literature, foreign languages, literature seminars, history of music, natural sciences, principles of medical treatment, history of female studies, history of blind people's literature and braille, handicraft practice, acupuncture, massage, musical training."

People who agreed with Yuri's firm convictions volunteered to act as leaders and mentors.

As Yuri's workload increased, more and more often she found she was too busy to return to the house where Takeya and her children waited.

But, as it was The Sunlight Association Home that was keeping Yuri from her motherhood duties, they thought it couldn't be helped and her family continued to offer her their full support.

However, no matter how widely Yuri appealed for students, no applications were received.

"It's not necessary for everything to go perfectly from the beginning."

As always, it was Takeya who understood her best.

It was around this time that Yuri heard the news that her inspiration, Helen Keller, would visit Japan.

Yuri prayed that somehow she would be able to meet Helen.

P20

In the beginning, Yuri knew that Helen had overcome 3 major disabilities, but she was unaware of the various activities Helen was involved in:
• movements to advance welfare for disabled people
• movements to press for women's liberation
• movements to advocate for world peace and anti-war activities

When she learned about such activities, the awe in which she held Helen was of a completely different dimension.

However, at the same time she felt a major conflict arising in her.

"I want to meet Helen and hear what she has to say."

"But she's completely different to me, carrying out her activities at a much higher level."

"A person acting to bring about goodwill between nations."

"She's bringing a hand-written letter from President Roosevelt in an attempt to ease the worsening relations between Japan and America."

"I can't possibly say I want to meet such a person privately."

"But, even so, I'm convinced Helen will understand what is necessary for the education of blind girls in Japan."

With this conflict in her heart, Yuri went to Osaka to meet Iwahashi Takeo, who had arranged Helen Keller's visit to Japan.

Iwahashi, a notable contributor to society, had become blind when he was a student.

Actually, in order to raise funds for the Blind Girls' High School and to publicize it, Yuri had decided to put on a music recital.

Yuri met Mr. Iwahashi and told him of her long held admiration for Helen, appealed to him for the need of the education of blind girls and explained how they intended to establish the Blind Girls' High School.

Mr. Iwahashi could see Yuri's enthusiasm and it was decided that he would get Helen to give a speech at Yuri's recital.

This news greatly excited the Sunlight Association Home.

"Helen Keller is coming to the concert!!"

For the next two months, any number of people, from Christian housewives to student volunteers, were constantly coming and going, all busy preparing for "An Evening of Music and a Speech by Helen Keller".

P22

On April 29th 1937, Yuri gave a speech to open the "Evening of Music and a Speech by Helen Keller".

"What is really pitiable in Japanese blind people's society is that there is nobody who is truly able to envision the future for blind people here. On this occasion, please give your generous support to us."

At about the halfway point of the recital, Helen Keller made her entrance to the accompaniment of a song played on the koto, entitled "A Song Dedicated to Miss Helen Keller".

The lyrics to this song had been written by Yuri. The packed room, with many people standing, all joined in to accompany Miyagi Michio, the composer and koto player, and sang along to Yuri's poem.

"A legend in other countries. From far away, we have yearned for this dream."

By touching her assistant's mouth and lips, Helen

was able to comprehend the words to the song.
In a quiet voice, she spoke softly from her place on the stage.
"One of my aims in visiting Japan is for people who suffer the same fate as me and live in darkness and silence, to discover meaning in their lives by being blessed and stepping out into the world of light. I want there to appear from among you someone such as Anne Sullivan to extend the hand of kindness to those who live in the dark."
The koto recital continued after that, the music melting into the gentle spring night.

The recital was a great success, but there were problems lurking in the background.
One of the main problems was that, on the day of the recital they were informed that the proceeds from the evening should be offered as a contribution to the cost of arranging Helen's visit to Japan.
Mr. Iwahashi had been unaware of this plan, but it seems that behind the demand was someone who was unhappy at Helen being used to attract funds to establish the Blind Girls' High School.
Of course, Yuri fully understood that Helen was working to establish goodwill between Japan and America. She also recognized that her personal desire to meet Helen wasn't appropriate, so she had listened to Helen's speech simply as one member of the audience.

P23

In the end, the evening made no contribution to the Blind Girls' High School project.
They had seen the recital as the first step in preparing for the School's establishment, but had failed and, in the end, Yuri's plan came to a complete standstill.
Moreover, there was a further disappointment for her. This time, it was somebody who had hoped for the establishment of the High School who complained that the proceeds from the recital had been used for another purpose.

P24

The air raids on Tokyo increasingly became more intense.
Being unable to take part in air defense drills, groups consisting mainly of blind people were viewed as a burden by the neighborhood associations.
And the existence of the Sunlight Association Home, which would easily burn down if fire broke out, was a particular thorn in their side.
Eventually, they received notification from the police to immediately close the Home and disperse to other places.
People who had families or carers to return had left, but, finally there remained 4 people with nowhere else to go.
"I don't mind dying here. Please let us stay beside you."
Having been begged like this by her students, Yuri appealed to graduates of the Home and suitable readers of Braille Club for places to stay. But no prospects for evacuation arose and the situation was desperate.
Just as she was about to give up, a small shrine in Oidaira village near to Lake Hamana in Shizuoka was offered as an evacuation site and Yuri and the others left Tokyo.
Yuri escaped from Tokyo, but Takeya remained behind.

P25

The shrine was located half way up a mountain, reached by a steep flight of 70 steps.
Life was tough for Yuri and the 4 blind students in this unfamiliar place. Even just gathering material to burn was a difficult task for them. Backing up the sloping face of the mountain, they gathered fallen leaves and dead wood and placed them in small baskets they carried on their backs.
And yet, the villagers couldn't just stand by and do nothing as they saw this strange group of evacuees. They gave them vegetables and a portion of their rice rations. These things were all thanks to the treatment skills that Yuri's group held.
For the old people in the village, massage was greatly appreciated.
"Ah, my old wife's back is really painful, won't you come and give her a massage?"

However, after a year there, they were forced to move on and in 1945, they took shelter from the wind and rain in a tobacco drying shed in a neighboring village.

P26

The war ended on August 15, 1945, but it wasn't at all easy for Yuri's group to return to Tokyo.
Their hardships continued.
On the contrary, the biggest hardship of Yuri's life befell her.
Yuri learned that Takeya had died in an unforeseen accident.
She left the other evacuees and headed for Tokyo in a state of despair, unable to believe that Takeya was dead.

A scorched stench hung in the air of Tokyo, the streets underfoot were strewn with rubble and Yuri was at a loss as to how to advance even one step
"Takeya isn't dead, it's a lie. If I get back to the house he'll be waiting there."
Firmly believing this, somehow Yuri managed to reach the house where Takeya had been living.
The house had survived the air raids.
"Takeya isn't here...... Maybe he's at the Sunlight Association Home...," thought Yuri.
The Home was still there as it had always been. In the rooms, damaged braille books were stacked in bundles.
However, Takeya wasn't there.

P27

Running her hands over the dusty braille books, Yuri mumbled to herself,
"Ah, it's all like a dream. Takeya is gone, too. I'm so sorry. You gave me the freedom to do what I wanted."
Apologizing over and over, she ripped up the braille books and burned the pages, unable to stop herself.
As Yuri mourned the loss of Takeya, the power to live seemed to drain from her body.
Her second son, who had been a student at Rikkyo University, had gone to the front and been killed in the war.
Finally, it seemed that the strange force that had saved her from the well so long ago was no longer there.

Yuri and her third daughter, Miwa, took up residence on the second floor of the Home. Her two elder daughters, Kumi and Michi, were already married and living elsewhere.
The popular tune "Song of the Apple" could be heard everywhere in the streets of Tokyo.
Japan was emerging from a long, dark tunnel and many Japanese were beginning to allow a sense of hope to grow at having survived the war.

About one year had passed since Takeya had died and it was New Year of 1947.
Yuri was suffering from a terrible cold and was confined to bed. She was running a high fever.
"I was a stubborn old woman, wasn't I?" she said to Miwa.
"What are you talking about?"
"It was wrong of me to be so conceited and want to study like that."
She ignored the concern in Miwa's voice.
"Dying doesn't bother me. It's just my body that will be gone, my spirit will always be here with each of you. That's all......."

P28

Throughout Yuri's last night, her daughter Miwa sat with her.
Struggling to breathe, she asked, "How many hours is it until dawn?"
"It's 4 o'clock now so it should be light in about two hours," Miwa answered.
"Do I still have 2 more hours?"
Suddenly, Yuri started repeating over and over, "Red---poppy---flower---juice, red---poppy---flower---juice."
"What? What do you want to say?" asked Miwa.
"Nothing. I just wanted to try saying it. I was thinking that if I chewed the petals of a deep red poppy it might ease the pain in my chest," she said in a surprisingly clear voice.
"When are redpoppies in bloom, I wonder?"
"Around May time. That's quite soon, we'll see them together, for sure."
"No, I won't make it to May. Ah, there's a mass of redpoppies in bloom! I can hear such beautiful music."

Miwa was silent and just watched her closely.
"This...is...my....Father's...world......."
Yuri haltingly sung a hymn. In the pale light her face was full of joy.
"Mother, mother, don't leave me!"
There was no answer.
Yuri's 55 years of life came to an end.

In America, red poppies were a symbol of remembrance for those killed in battle.

P29

Isn't it very probable that Yuri regretted she didn't get to meet Helen?
If she had had really tried, her wish to meet Helen that evening would have come true.
The reason she didn't dare to do so could be that she wouldn't have been able to meet Helen in the way she had imagined, both of them touching each other's face.
A letter that Yuri received from Helen said the following:

"How truly dark are the minds of we warriors. Opportunities are snatched away through fear, the opportunity to overcome the obstacles of this world, to be victorious through the power of will."

It seems that Helen had completely understood how Yuri had struggled.
In 1948, the year after Yuri passed away, a new education law was signed under which a system of compulsory education for blind, deaf and dumb children was established.

P31

And that year, Helen travelled to Japan again.
She visited Hiroshima and Nagasaki and said the following:
"The scenes there were truly shocking. Though the people were struggling in agony, they didn't mention their own injuries. My soul has never been so moved."

Helen managed to visit Japan for a third time in 1955.
People throughout Japan are aware of Helen's activities.
In comparison, Saito Yuri's life and efforts have been completely unknown.
Yuri's two elder daughters weren't able to be with her when she left this world, but they went on to live their lives clearly following Yuri's beliefs.
Miwa, her third daughter who was present at her death, went on to be an actress. In 1994, the "Life of Saito Yuri Production Committee" was formed and the movie "Light for Visually Impaired People! The Life of the Blind Woman Saito Yuri" was completed.
Saito Yuri has truly left her mark on history. Books have been published. And also a picture book.....

©Nobby Kealey 2018,Printed in Japan,Published by Ounkai

1902年にヘレン・ケラーが書いた『わたしの生涯』を読んだ小つるは、ヘレンが自分とは真逆で、とても裕福な家庭で非常に甘やかされて育ったことを知りました。
・ヘレンは、1880年生まれでわたしより11歳上。
・同じように病気で目が見えなくなったのね。
・でも、耳も聞こえない！
・話せない！！
・どういうことなの？
・聞こえないというのは自分の声も聞こえない。
・自分が出している音もわからない、
・しゃべることなんかできるわけがない。
　小つるは、そう思うとヘレンのことが気になってしかたありません。いつもヘレンと出会う日を想像していました。

　小つるはヘレンの顔にふれる。ヘレンも小つるにさわる。ヘレンは耳が聞こえないぶん、よりしっかり小つるの顔をさぐる……。

　小つるは、こういうことも知りました。
・ヘレンの両親は、電話の発明者として知られるグラハム・ベルをよく知っていた。
・ベルが紹介してくれたマサチューセッツ州の盲学校の校長先生が、卒業生の当時20歳のアン・サリバンをヘレンの家庭教師に派遣。
・小さいころから弱視だったサリバン先生は、自らの経験を活かしてヘレンに指文字や言葉、そしてわがまま放題だったヘレンをしつけた。
・ある日ヘレンは、手にかかる冷たい何かが「水」というもので、それを文字で表すと「WATER」と書くことを理解した。
・口を動かして、「ウォーター」と発音することも、サリバン先生から教えられた。
・これがきっかけとなり、ヘレンは、すべてのものに名前があること、口をそれぞれに適切に動かすことで、自分の思ったことを他人に知らせることができることを知った。

　ヘレンは、1890年にはボストンの聾学校で声の出し方を学びます。
　1894年には、ニューヨーク聾学校に入学し、さらに発声練習にはげみます。
　小つるが生まれたのは、そのころでした。そして、ヘレンと同様に病気で、光を失ってしまったのです。
　ヘレンは1900年10月、ラドクリフ・カレッジ（現ハーバード大学）に入学します。

　3年間の代用教員の生活ののち、小つるの才能を認めた森院長は、岐阜訓盲院の派遣生として小つるを東京盲学校師範科の鍼按科に入学させました。
　派遣費用は、寄付や在宅治療の謝礼金などでまかなわれました。
　そうまでして小つるを東京に派遣する森院長の小つるへの期待は、はかりしれないほど大きいものでした。

　東京盲学校での生活は、小つるにとって夢のような時間でした。
　同級生は全部で9名。男子学生7名、女子学生は小つるを入れて、たったの2名。みんな全国の盲学校から派遣された、優秀な人材でした。それぞれに学校を将来牽引していくと見込まれた人たちです。

　この間に、小つるは「英和辞典」の写本を仕上げました。
　全部で8冊、その1冊1冊にペンネームを打ちそえました。
　White Lily
　そうです。あのときの真っ白い百合です。

「盲女子の結婚はいかなる場合でも望ましいものではない。盲女子は、妻として、母としても、その義務を完全に果たすことができないからである。もし結婚しようとしたなら警告して結婚させないようにするべきである」

これは『盲教育学』という本に書かれていたことです。

しかし、これに対しては、すでに幅広い教養を身につけて、アメリカをはじめとする世界の事情にも通じていた小つるが抵抗するのは、無理のないことでした。

小つるは、
（人はみんな平等。違いを認めながらも助け合うことが大切だわ）
と、思っていたのですから。

そんな小つるが恋をしました。
相手は、東京盲学校の二級下の斎藤武弥でした。武弥は、全盲の小つるとは違って、弱視でした。

1913年、時代は明治から大正にかわっていました。小つるは東京盲学校の卒業を迎えます。

岐阜訓盲院の派遣生として全額給費で東京に来ていた小つるは、訓盲院に戻り、指導者になることが求められていました。

そこで、小つるはとんでもないことを考え、そして実行したのです。

それは、武弥の「鍼按免許証」を取りあげることです。

「これが婚約の印よ」

小つるはそういって、武弥の免許証を岐阜へ持ち帰ってしまったのです。

武弥に会えなくなる不安からの強引なやりかたでした。

久しぶりの訓盲院でした。

森院長にとっても生徒たちにとっても東京帰りの小つるが放つ空気は、とても華やかです。

みんなは、小つるが東京で得てきたものに触れたいという大きな期待で、わくわくしていました。

このため、小つるの話は、みんなを愕然とさせてしまいます。

「わたしは、東京盲学校でいっしょだった斎藤武弥さんと結婚の約束をしました」

「どういうことかな？」

と、言葉こそおだやかで落ち着いていたものの、小つるの指導者としての資質に訓盲院の将来を託そうと考えていた森院長は動揺していました。

でも、小つるには、それが見えません。

「自分勝手なのはわかっています。先生、どうか許してください。わたしは、どうしても斎藤さんと結婚したいのです」

まっすぐに一点にむかって話す小つるの強い語調からは、相当の決意が伝わってきました。

しかし、森院長は小つるの激しさに気づきながらも、小つるの表情を見ることはできませんでした。小つるの気迫に押され、結婚を許すほかありませんでした。

結婚を認めてもらった小つるは、1913年から2年間、これまでの感謝を込めて、岐阜訓盲院のために寸暇を惜しまず働きました。

そうして1915年秋、東京の病院でマッサージ師をしていた斎藤武弥と結婚。東京雑司ヶ谷の新居で新生活をスタートしました。

この結婚を機に、小つるは、斎藤百合と名のるようになりました。

　ごく当たり前の家庭生活を全く知らずに育った百合にとって、武弥との生活は、慣れない家事に四苦八苦しながらも、新鮮で、毎日が幸せそのものでした。

　買い物に行く道、銭湯への道、東京の込み入った道にも慣れてきました。たまに武弥を迎えにいく駅への道にもすっかり慣れて、街を一人でも不安なく歩けるようになりました。

　そうして、百合は、まもなく子どもを授かりました。
そんなある日のことでした。

「女按摩さんかい。お腹の子は誰の子だえ」
　すれ違いざまに耳元で聞こえた男の声には、さげすんだような笑いがまざっていました。
　百合はふらつきそうになる足元に力を入れなおし、やっとの思いで家にたどりつきました。
「ごめんね。ごめんね」
　百合は泣きながら、まだ見ぬわが子にあやまりつづけ、お腹をさする手を止めることができませんでした。
（わたしが目が見えないせいで、赤ちゃんまでがばかにされる。わたしはいい。
でも、赤ちゃんには、本当に申しわけない）

　そこへ武弥が帰ってきました。
「百合、何かあったのか？」
　百合は、思わず武弥にしがみつくと、涙が一気にほおを伝っていきました。
　事情を聞いた武弥はいいました。
「いいかい、百合、お腹の赤ちゃんは、ぼくと百合の希望なんだ。
これからの社会の希望でもあるんだ」
　百合は、黙って、大きくうなずきました。
「世の中の盲女性のなかには、親の名前をいうことができない人がいるのは、確かだ。

だからこそ、ぼくたちは、しっかりとこの子を育てていかなければならないんだ。盲女性に対する、社会の偏見を変えなければならないんだ。
しっかりしてください。新米おかあさん」
　そういいながら、武弥は百合のお腹にフゥと息をかけました。それは温かく、百合の体と心に沁み入っていったようです。
　このことを機に、百合は、盲女性のおかれた社会的地位の低さについて深く考えるようになりました。
　1916年8月、百合は、長女久美を出産しました。

百合にとって、弱視の武弥が虫眼鏡を使って読んでくれる朝の30分の新聞のニュースは、大切な情報源でした。社会の窓口です。

ある日の朝のニュースが、百合の人生を大きく変えることになりました。

「1918年に東京女子大学開校。キリスト教精神にのっとり、女性の高等教育をめざす」

「えっ、もう一度読んで」

百合は興奮を隠せませんでした。

「でも、わたしなんかには関係ないことね。無理よね。だって、もう26歳だし、……。何より目が見えないんだもの……。しかも、子どももいて……。学費を払うことができないし……」

百合は、自分を納得させるように、自分の悪条件をあげつらねています。はじめの興奮も、さめていきます。

「最初からあきらめることないだろう。詳しく調べてみよう」

と、武弥に背中を押されて、百合は、願書を取り寄せることになりました。

試験は、口頭試問でした。面接官は、後に東京女子大学第二代学長となった安井てつでした。

「ここは、学問を志す子女が集う学び舎です。あなたはすでに結婚していて、母親でもあります。それに、目が不自由。それでも学問についてこられると思っているのですか？」

開口一番の厳しい問いかけは、百合を発奮させました。

「たとえ盲人であっても、教育の機会は平等であるべきです。盲女性の社会的地位を向上させるためには、高等教育を受けられる人を増やしていく必要があります。

まず、わたしにその機会をお与えください」

百合は開き直ったように訴えました。そのため、

「あーあ、失敗してしまった」

と、合格をあきらめていました。ところが、その数日後、合格通知が届いたのです。

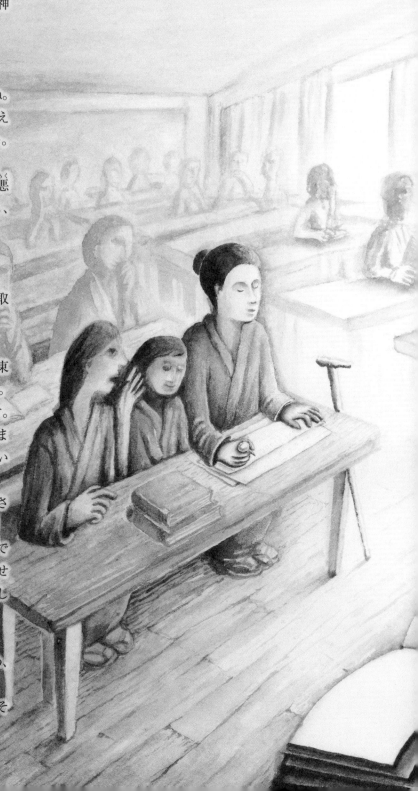

東京女子大学の初代学長は、自ら「太平洋の架け橋となる」と国際平和に魂を捧げた新渡戸稲造で、障害者に対して深い理解をもっていました。百合の熱意が通じたのです。安井てつの厳しい言葉も、百合の覚悟を確認するためのものでした。
「わたしが大学にいける!」
その後、安井は百合のより良き理解者として、百合の活動を支えていきます。

大学の講堂での百合の座席はいつも一番前でした。講義の内容を聞きもらさないように、ひたすら点字でメモする姿はクラスメイトにとって新鮮な感動でした。点字を見たことのない人が多かった時代、近くで点字を打っているのを見るのですから。
黒板に書かれた文字は隣の席の人が読み上げてくれることもありました。
百合はたちまち大学で人気もの。
それにしても、子どもを背負ったり、隣の席にちょこんと座らせながらの受講に対し、みんな寛容に協力してくれたのは、百合の人柄によるところも大きかったのでしょう。

卒業が近づいてきましたが、百合にはもっと勉強したいことがありました。英語です。
百合は1923年、英文学科に編入しました。
ところが、その年の9月1日、関東大震災が発生。震災後、変わり果てた東京の街は百合の足元にはとても危険で、退学を余儀なくされました。
それでも、百合は1925年に東京盲学校研究科英文科に入学して勉学を続けました。武弥も仕事をしながら夜学に通って社会政策を学んでいました。
当然ながら家計は火の車です。それでも夫婦ともに天性の明るさから、人の出入りが頻繁で、にぎやかな暮らしぶりでした。
学ぶことで、盲人やあらゆる障害者の社会的地位の向上を実現しようとしていた二人にとって、子育ては、学業を我慢する理由にならなかったのです。

武弥の東京盲学校時代からの友人の一人に、ロシア人のワシリー・エロシェンコがいました。
日本で盲人が鍼や按摩の技術で自立できている現状を視察しに来日した彼には、幅広い交友関係がありました。

彼に誘われて、武弥と百合が参加したサロンでは、毎回、芸術家や文学者が集まり、新しい時代を求めて議論が白熱していました。
時には彼のバイオリンに合わせて、百合もオルガンを弾いて楽しい歌の輪ができました。

　しかし、大正デモクラシーといわれた時代です。警察の取り締まりが厳しいなかでのこうした集会は、建物の閉塞感と心の開放感とが交錯するなんとも不思議な空間でした。
　エロシェンコは、危険思想の人物とみなされ、国外追放されます。それは、二人がいっしょに復活祭のミサに出席した翌日のことでした。
　そうしたなか、盲人の社会的地位の向上をめざし、二人は家計をやりくりして多くの点字本を自費出版しつづけました。

1928年11月には、百合は武蔵野婦人会（のち陽光婦人会）を組織します。ついで1930年には、盲女子のため陽光会を開設しました。
　その理念は、こうでした。
「わたしには太陽は見えないけれど、太陽は世界じゅうの人びとを照らす。盲人が社会の隅にいてはいけない。盲人でも平等に教育を受けられる社会にしなければならない」
　陽光会の運営は、武弥が立ち上げた季刊誌『点字倶楽部』がたよりでした。文芸・盲人問題・時事問題・読者からの投稿など内容が多岐にわたっていたこの雑誌は、とくに地方に住む盲人たちにとって貴重な読み物で、到着を楽しみにしている人が増えていきました。
　百合は、さらに精力的！　1935年12月には、豊島区雑司ヶ谷の古い一軒家の玄関に「陽光会ホーム」という真新しい看板を掲げたのです。東京女子大学学長の安井てつなど、多くの支援者が百合を支えました。日本点字図書館の初代館長となった本間一夫もその一人です。
　『点字倶楽部』の編集もホームでおこないました。コトコト点字を打つ音、ガッシャン、ガッシャンと印刷機の音が響いています。学生ボランティアの音読や若い人たちの笑い声が、粗末な二階家から聞こえてきます。
「こちらは何の家ですか？」
と、立ち止まってのぞきこむ人もいました。
　そこは、若い盲女性のための学びの家です。
　百合は、岐阜聖公会訓盲院の森院長との出会いによって人生が開けました。森院長が百合に与えた愛情を、今度は百合が、これから出会う盲女性に与える番です。
　ところが、そこに集まる人が増えてくると、ホームを維持していくには『点字倶楽部』の発行だけでは厳しくなってきました。
　点字器や用紙、治療用具の取次販売をおこなって、運営費をまかなおうとしました。
　そんななかでも、百合を頼りに地方から上京する人が後をたちません。百合は、そういう人たちにホームを宿として、食事も提供し、温かくもてなすのです。
　百合が「盲女子の母」とよばれるのは、こうしたことによります。
　そんなホームの玄関先には、山茶花の古木がみごとな花をいっぱい咲かせていました。

　1936年、2・26事件が勃発。1937年7月7日、盧溝橋事件勃発。日中間で全面戦争がはじまります。
　日本の社会は悪くなる一方。そんななかでも百合の理想は変わりません。
「晴眼者と肩を並べて働く女性の姿を見たい。そのためには20年、30年先のリーダーを育てなければ！」
　いつしか「盲女子高等学園」という学校の夢が育っていきます。
　百合は、1937年12月の『点字倶楽部』に「盲女子高等学園の生徒募集」の記事を大きく掲載しました。
「盲女子社会の中核になるべき者の養成を目的とします。教授科目：西洋哲学史、国文学史、外国語、文学演習、音楽史、自然科学、医療要綱、女性科学史、盲人文化史及び点字、手芸演習、鍼・按・音楽実習」
　百合の強い思いに賛同した人たちが、ボランティアで指導役を買ってでてくれました。
　仕事は増える一方、百合はあまりの忙しさに、武弥と子どもたちの待つ家にはなかなか帰れませんでした。
　でも、母親が取られたところが陽光会ホームならしかたないと、家族みんなで百合を支えつづけていました。
　ところが百合が広げた両手に飛び込んでくる盲女子は、まったくいませんでした。
「最初から上手くいくはずないよ」
　いつでも武弥が、一番の理解者でした。

　百合の憧れのヘレン・ケラーが来日するというニュースを知ったのは、そのころでした。
　百合は、何としてもヘレンに会いたいと願ったのです。

当初の百合は、ヘレンが三重苦を克服したことを知っていましたが、ヘレンがおこなっていたさまざまな活動については知りませんでした。
・障害者の福祉向上のために活動
・婦人の解放を願って活動
・平和と反戦を唱えて活動
　こうした活動を知った百合は、ヘレンに対して、それまでとはまったく次元のことなる畏敬の念を抱いていたのです。
　しかし、それと同時にこんな大きな葛藤も生じました。
（ヘレンに会いたい、話を聞きたい）
（でも、わたしなんかと違って、はるかに高いところで活動をしている人。国と国との親善活動をしている人）
（険悪になった日米関係をときほぐす親善大使として、アメリカのルーズベルト大統領の親書を携えてやってくる）
（そんな立派な人に個人的に会いたいなどといえない）
（それでも、ヘレンなら日本の盲女子の教育の必要性をわかってくれるに違いない）
　そうした葛藤を胸に、百合はヘレン・ケラーの来日を実現させた岩橋武夫に会うために大阪へ行きました。
　岩橋は社会事業家で、学生時代に失明した人でした。

　実は、盲女子高等学園を何としてもつくりたかった百合は、その宣伝と資金集めの目的で、音楽会を開く計画を立てていたのです。
　百合は岩橋に会って、募らせてきたヘレンへの熱い思いを語り、盲女子の教育の必要性を訴え、自分たちがつくろうとしている盲女子高等学園についても説明しました。

　百合の熱意は岩橋に通じました。岩橋の仲介でヘレンが音楽会で講演してくれることが決まったのです。
　陽光会ホームでは、蜂の巣をつついたような大騒ぎになりました。
（ヘレン・ケラーが音楽会にきてくれる！）
　それからの２か月間、ホームはクリスチャンの婦人たち、ボランティアの学生など、さまざまな人たちが入れかわりたちかわりやってきて、「ヘレンの講演と音楽の夕べ」の準備に大忙しでした。

1937年4月29日「ヘレンの講演と音楽の夕べ」は、百合の挨拶からはじまりました。
「日本の盲人社会で本当に悲しむべきことは、真に盲人社会の未来を示してくれる人がいないことです。今日のよき機会に、わたくしどもにあたたかな愛の手をおさしのべください」
　会も中盤にさしかかったとき、「ヘレン・ケラー女子に捧ぐる歌」の箏曲演奏と共にヘレン・ケラーが入場してきました。
　この曲の歌詞は、百合が作詞したものでした。立ち見が出るほど大勢の人たちが、作曲家で箏曲演奏家である宮城道雄の奏でる箏の音に合わせて「百合の詩」を歌い、一つになりました。
「とつくにの　遠きかなたの　かたり草
　いくとせながき　憧れのゆめ」
　ヘレンは介助者の唇に触れて、その歌詞を読み取っていました。壇上でゆっくりと静かに語りました。
「わたしが日本を訪問した目的の一つは、わたしと同じ運命にある闇と沈黙のうちに住む友が、恵を得て光の世界に踊りでて、人生の意義を発見することです。皆様のなかからもサリバンのような人が現れ、闇の中にいる人に愛の手をさしのべていただきたい」
　その後も箏の演奏がつづき、春の夜に溶け込んでいきました。

　こうして音楽会は成功しましたが、その陰には苦難がありました。
　それは、会の当日になって、会の収益金をヘレンの歓迎事業に寄付するようにいわれたことに象徴されます。
　岩橋も知らないことでしたが、そういった要求の背景には、ヘレンが百合の盲女子高等学園の資金集めに利用されるのはおかしいという見方の人がいたことは確かでしょう。
　もちろん百合は、ヘレンが日本とアメリカの親善のために活動している人であることを十分にわかっていました。ヘレンに会いたいという個人的な気持ちをもつのもよくないと思い、ヘレンの講演を一聴衆として聞いたのです。

この会は、盲女子高等学園の計画に寄与できませんでした。
そして百合の学園構想は、設立準備の第一歩と位置づけていたこの会でつまずいてしまい、結局、頓挫してしまいました。
しかも、百合の落胆には、さらなる追い打ちがありました。
今度は、盲女子高等学園の設立を願っていた人たちのなかに、会の収益金が別に使われたことに不満をいう人が出てきたのです。

東京の空襲も激しさを増してきました。
　隣組の人たちは、防空訓練にも参加できない、盲人ばかりの集団を迷惑がるようになります。
　火を出したらあっけなく燃えてしまいそうな陽光会ホームの存在は、もはや目の上のたんこぶ。
　ついに、警察から「至急解散してどこかへいくように」といった通達を受けました。
　家族や引き取り手のある者は帰っていき、どこにも行き場のない４人だけが残りました。
「もうここで死んでもいいから、
　先生のそばにおいてください」
　そう懇願された百合は、ホームの「卒業生」や『点字倶楽部』のめぼしい読者に頼んだりしました。しかし、疎開先の目途は立たず、絶望的でした。
　あきらめかけたころ、浜名湖の奥の大平村の小さなお宮が疎開場所として提供されることになり、百合たちは、東京をはなれました。
　百合は、武弥を東京に残して疎開することにしました。

お宮は、かなり高い山の中腹の、70あまりの急な階段をあがったところにありました。

知らない場所で盲人4人だけの百合の疎開生活は凄まじいものでした。火種を集めるだけでもひと苦労です。山の斜面をあとずさりしながら落ち葉や枯れ木を拾い、背負った小さなかごに入れてゆきます。

それでも、この一風変わった疎開者たちに、村人たちは配給米をわけてくれたり、野菜を差し入れしてくれたり……。それは、百合たちの治療技術のおかげでした。

村の年寄りたちにとって、按摩はとてもありがたいことだったのです。

「ばあちゃんが背中、痛がっているんだ。来て按摩やってもらえねぇか」

しかし、そこも1年ほどで立ち退きを強いられることになり、1945年には、百合たちはその隣村の煙草の乾燥室を借りて雨風をしのいでいました。

　1945年8月15日終戦。
　でも、百合たちは、そうたやすく東京にもどることができないでいました。
　苦難は続きます。
　それどころか、人生最大の苦難がやってきます。
　武弥が不慮の事故で死亡したという知らせ。
　武弥が死んだなんて信じられない百合は、死に物狂いで疎開先から東京へ。

　東京の街は、焼け焦げたような臭いが漂い、足元はがれきだらけで、一歩踏みだすだけでも途方に暮れてしまいそう。
　(武弥が死んだなんて、うそだ。家にもどれば、武弥がまっている)
　そう信じて、なんとか武弥が暮らしていた家にたどりつきます。
　その家は、空襲をまぬがれていました。
　(武弥はいない……。もしかしたら陽光会ホームの方に……)
　陽光会ホームは、その形をとどめていました。
　部屋には、破れかけた点字本が束になって積まれています。
　しかし、武弥はいません。

　百合は、ほこりをかぶった点字本にさわりながら、つぶやきました。
「ああ、すべて幻のよう」
「もう、武弥さんも逝ってしまった。ごめんなさい。
ずっとしたいようにさせていただきました」
「ごめんなさい」を繰り返しながら、点字本を破いては燃やし、破いては燃やし、その手は止まることがありませんでした。
　このときの百合は、武弥を失った喪失感で、体から生きる気力が奪われていました。
　立教大学にいった次男が出征して戦死。
　すでにあのときの何か不思議な力は、なくなってしまったのでしょうか。

　百合はホームの二階で、三女の美和とともに生活をはじめます。長女の久美、次女の美知は、結婚してはなれて暮らしていました。
　東京の街には『リンゴの唄』が流れています。日本じゅうが真っ暗だったトンネルから抜け出し、多くの日本人が戦後の復興に希望を膨らませはじめていました。

　武弥が亡くなって1年ほどが過ぎた1947年の正月のことでした。
　百合は風邪をこじらせて寝込んでしまいました。すごい熱です。
「わたしは頑固なおばさんだったね」
と、百合は美和にいいました。
「何をいってるの？」
「生意気に勉強したからいけなかった」
　心配する美和をよそに、
「わたし、死ぬことなんて何でもありゃしない。体がなくなるだけで、魂はみんなのまわりにうろうろしているからね。ただね……」

最期の夜、そばにいたのは三女の美和でした。
百合は荒い苦しそうな息をしながら
「あと何時間で夜が明けるかい？」
「今4時だから、あと2時間で明るくなるわ」
「まだ2時間もあるのかい」
百合は、とつぜん、
「レッド ポピー フラワー ジュース、レッド ポピー フラワー ジュース」
と、何度となく繰り返しました。
「何？　何か伝えたいの？」
と、美和。
「ただ、そう言ってみたかった。真っ赤なポピーの花びらをかみしめたら、胸が苦しいのが治るだろうと思ってね」
驚くほどはっきりした声です。
「レッドポピーの花は、いつ咲くのかしらねぇ」

「5月ごろよ。もうすぐよ、きっといっしょに見られるわよ」
「5月じゃとても間に合わないねえ。あぁ、レッドポピーの花が咲き乱れているわ。美しい音楽が聞こえてくる」
美和は、だまって見守っているだけでした。
「ここも、かみの、みくになれば……」
百合はとぎれとぎれに讃美歌を歌っています。
淡い光の中で、百合の顔は幸福そのものです。
「お母さん、逝かないで！」
返事はありません。
そして百合は55年の生涯を閉じました。

レッドポピーは、アメリカなどで戦没者に手向けられる花だといわれています。

もしかすると百合は、ヘレンに会えなかったことが心残りだったのでしょうか。

あの夕べ、百合はヘレンに会おうとすれば、それもかなったのです。

そのとき、あえてそうしなかったのは、百合が思い描いていたヘレンとの対面―お互いに顔に触れあう―を実現できなかったからかもしれません。

後日、ヘレンからもらった手紙には、こう書かれていました。

まことに暗い強者どもの心。
かくて障害者からその好機を奪う。
地上の束縛を克服し、
精神力のうちに勝利しようとする好機を。

ヘレンは百合の苦悩をすべてわかっていたのかもしれません。

百合が亡くなった翌年の1948年、盲・聾唖児の就学義務制を定めた、新しい学校教育法が公布されました。

そして、その年、ヘレンが再び来日。
ヘレンは広島、長崎を訪れ、こういいました。
「それは本当にショッキングな光景でした。人々は苦しみにもがきながらも、自分たちの傷については何もいいませんでした。これほどまでに魂をゆさぶられたことはありません」

ヘレンは1955年に三度目の来日を果たしました。
ヘレンのこうした活動は、日本じゅうの人に知られています。
それにくらべて、斎藤百合の生涯と活躍は、まったく知られていませんでした。
長女と次女は、百合の旅立ちには間に合いませんでしたが、百合の意思をついでしっかりと人生を歩んでいきました。
百合を看取った三女の美和は、その後女優になり、1994年には、「斎藤百合の生涯製作委員会」を結成し、『視覚障害者に光を！ 盲目の斎藤百合の生涯』という映画を完成させました。
斎藤百合もちゃんと歴史に足跡を残しました。本も出されました。そして絵本も……。

あとがき

　本書は、今から127年前に誕生した一人の視覚障害のある女性、斎藤百合の一生をもとにしてつくった絵本です。

　彼女は、障害者に対する差別と偏見があたりまえの時代に、視覚障害のある女性の社会的地位を高めるためには、何をすべきかを考え、女子大学へ進学し、苦難のなかで多くのことを学びました。しかも子育てをしながら。今とは異なり、大学へ進学できたのは、一握りの人だけ。どれほどの苦労があったことか……。彼女は、視覚障害のある女性が自由に学び、働くことができる施設として陽光会ホームを設立。差別や偏見に負けずに、女性の職業自立を実践し、今日の女性の教育、社会的地位の向上への基礎をつくりました。

　一方、同時代を生きた女性としては、アメリカ人のヘレン・ケラーがいます。ヘレンの功績は、誰もが知るところですが、知名度が高いのは、活躍の場が世界であったことと、幾多の絵本で紹介されたことが大きいでしょう。でも、もし斎藤百合の絵本が、もっと早くに世に出ていたら……と。

　今回の絵本では、小島伸吾さんの描かれた絵の濃淡は、当時の世相を反映し、タケシタナカさんのたんたんとした文体が、かえって斎藤百合の生涯をドラスティックに読者に伝えてくれます。

　彼女の一生を知ることで、一人でも多くの方々と感動を共有できたら、たいへんうれしく思います。

　末筆ながら本書の刊行にあたりましては、小学館、一般財団法人日本児童教育振興財団より、ご支援を賜わりましたことに厚く御礼申し上げます。その他、制作に関わって頂いた全ての方々に感謝申し上げます。

2018年3月1日
社会福祉法人　桜雲会

文／タケシタナカ
1953年東京都生まれ。本名、稲葉茂勝。編集者としてこれまで1100以上の作品を手がけ、自著は80冊以上。近年は子どもジャーナリストとして、また絵本ネームのタケシタナカで、大人の絵本を発表し続けている。

英訳／ノビ・キーリ（Nobby Kealey）
1957年イギリス・マンチェスター生まれ。シェフィールド大学にて日本語を専攻。来日後はカメラマンとして活躍する一方、英語教師のほか、数々のテレビCMに出演。松蔭学園イングリッシュ・スクール校長。

絵／小島伸吾
1967年愛知県生まれ。創形美術学校で絵を学び、イシス編集学校で編集工学を学ぶ。版画やタブローを中心に、創作活動および、編集とアートをつなげる多岐にわたる活動をしている。

監修／社会福祉法人　桜雲会
1892年、東京盲唖学校（現在の筑波大学附属視覚特別支援学校）の盲学生の同窓会として発足。1930年に最初の鍼按科教科書を出版。以後、医学専門書を中心に点字図書や録音図書、拡大図書の製作・販売をおこなう。

監修／馬場景子
愛知県生まれ。日本福祉大学講師。30年あまり、障碍者言語情報獲得の研究をおこなっている。長年、斎藤百合研究に携わってきた。

デザイン・DTP制作／
株式会社エヌ・アンド・エス企画（石井友紀）

> この図書は、一般財団法人　日本児童教育振興財団の助成により制作いたしました。

闇を照らした白い花　斎藤百合の生涯とヘレン・ケラー

2018年4月1日 初版発行　　　　　　　　　　　　　　　NDC289

発行者　　一幡良利
発行所　　社会福祉法人桜雲会
　　　　　〒169-0075 東京都新宿区高田馬場4-11-14-102
　　　　　電話　03-5337-7866
　　　　　http://ounkai.jp/
印刷・製本　瞬報社写真印刷株式会社

©Takeshita Naka, Shingo Kojima 2018, Printed in Japan, Published by Ounkai　　32P　210×260mm
ISBN978-4-904611-56-2 C0723

乱丁・落丁の場合は、お取り替えいたします。無断複写複製（コピー）は著作権法上での例外を除き禁じられています。